Rhymes Of Corporate Crimes

50 Verses from the Corner Office

Sheena Joseph

BookLeaf Publishing

India | USA | UK

Made with ❤ on the BookLeaf Publishing Platform
www.bookleafpub.in
www.bookleafpub.com

Dedication

To every person who has braved the boardroom, mastered the art of the perfect email (and the even more perfect "gentle reminder"), and navigated the labyrinth of KPIs, KRAs, and endless CC'd threads—this book is for you.

For the decades spent balancing ambition with patience, innovation with compliance, and strategic vision with the reality of office politics—your journeys through India's corporate giants are nothing short of inspiration.

This collection is a tribute to the whispered sighs in long meetings, the silent victories over impossible deadlines, and the countless cups of coffee that fueled resilience. It's an ode to the struggles, the satire, the soul-searching —and ultimately, the wisdom that emerges when you see the game for what it is.

May these verses bring knowing smiles, a few cathartic chuckles, and perhaps, a well-earned moment of reflection. And if nothing else, may they remind you that while corporate life may test you, it can for sure evolve you.

With admiration and a knowing nod, I Remain,

Sheena Joseph

Preface

The corporate life is a paradox—structured yet unpredictable, rewarding yet exhausting, filled with ambition yet often lacking meaning. For many, it's more than just a job; it's a stage where identities are shaped, struggles unfold, and victories—both grand and quiet—are earned. Some live to earn, others earn to live, but either way, the walls of corporate corridors shape much of our existence.

This book is a collection of poetry that seeks to make you think, guide you, and perhaps most importantly, help you find balance. These verses capture the highs and lows, the unspoken frustrations, and the silent triumphs of professional life. They ask questions that linger beyond boardrooms, challenge the status quo, and offer a fresh lens on the daily grind.

Whether you are a fresh recruit still learning the language of corporate emails, a seasoned executive who has seen it all, or someone searching for meaning amid endless meetings, these poems are for you. They are not just words on a page but echoes of every unanswered email, every strategic maneuver, and every dream tucked away between deadlines.

Let these poems be a mirror, a refuge, and perhaps even a guide as you navigate the complex, often amusing, and always evolving world of work. Because while the corporate machine may shape our days, it doesn't have to define our souls.

Welcome to *Rhymes of Corporate Crimes, 50 Verses from the Corner Office*.

Acknowledgements

To my mentors who led with wisdom and grace,
And the bosses who tested my patience and pace.
To my peers who stood like comrades in war,
And also the ones who made each task go so far.
To the teams that thrived, to those that fell,
To the coffee chats where stories swelled.
To cross-functional souls, the bridges they build,
In decks and deadlines, where our fate was sealed.
For lessons in kindness, in power, in spin,
For showing me losses, for teaching me wins.
To all I have met on this corporate ride,
May your tribe grow, may you thrive in your side!

1. Woman, What would you do if not afraid ?

Would you stand up in a room full of men,
Hold your ground, speak up again?
Would you argue your case like your life depends,
Not for a fight, but for what transcends?

Would you claim your space, take your due,
When they call you "too much" for simply being you?
Would you shatter the silence, break the mold,
Rewrite the stories that have long been told?

Would you voice your stand for feminism, bold,
Even when the room turns quiet and cold?
Would you face the stares, the disapproving nods,
And still walk forward against the odds?

Would you overcome the fear of not being liked,
Of whispers, judgments, power misused, spiked?
Would you trade approval for something more—
A life that's real, a self assured?

Because if you do, then you become true—
Not just to others, but first to you.
A force unshaken, a voice that stays,
A woman unbound in a world that sways.

2. Diversity is not just a number!

Diversity is not just a box you check,
Not a quota, nor a stat to collect.
It's the voices heard, the stories told,
The courage to break the single mold.

It's not just colors in a room,
Or names that vary in a Zoom.
It's thoughts that clash, then intertwine,
A richer truth in every line.

It's how we listen, how we grow,
How we unlearn what we thought we know.
It's lifting those long left behind,
A world rebuilt, just, and kind.

It's not just presence—it's a place,
At every table, in every space.
Not token words or empty sight,
But real inclusion, true and bright.

So count the numbers if you must,
But know that figures aren't enough.
For change is born when hearts expand—
Not just in tally, but in stand.
Not only in a position, but in a band...

3. Executive Presence - The Mantra

What is executive presence, they say,
A polished stance, a measured way?
A voice that carries, firm yet light,
A gaze that holds, a stance upright?

Is it a style, a practiced art,
A checklist made to set apart?
Or, is it a bias, thinly veiled,
A silent rule where few prevailed?

A cage of form, a crafted mold,
Where sameness reigns, where few are bold.
To speak, to lead, to claim the stage,
Yet bound within a quiet cage.

Where is the space for those who rise
In different ways, with different ties?
For some will lead with quiet grace,
And some will storm, will shake the place.

Be Trump, or be Obama, bold or refined,
Be Oprah's wisdom, or Kardashian's definition.
There is no single path, no single call—
We're vast enough to fit them all.

So own your space in your own way,
No rules to bend, no role to play.
For executive presence isn't one set mold,
But the truth within, that you make bold.

4. Team Marketing, Ohh!
Am I Just a Viral Post?

Am I just a viral post you chase,
A fleeting trend in the digital space?
A like, a share, a metric to boast,
A momentary blip, a forgotten ghost?

Am I the clickbait line you weave,
A clever hook to make them believe?
Do you see the story behind the screen,
The life, the purpose, the in-between?

You call it marketing, a craft, an art,
But where's the connection, the human part?
Is it just impressions and reach to gain,
Or does meaning still run in your vein?

Do you hear the voices behind the views,
The hopes, the doubts, the reasons they choose?
Or am I reduced to a campaign's thread,
A fleeting post in a newsfeed spread?

If all I am is engagement's score,
A trend you exploit, then nothing more,
Then tell me, where is the heart you claim,
The soul of marketing amidst the fame?

Look past the algorithms, beyond the charts,
Find the people, their minds, their hearts.
For I am more than the buzz you seek,
I ama human—authentic and unique.

So ask yourself—what do you really pursue,
If marketing forgets the human too?

5. It's performance time, HR, but am I just a Number?

Am I just a number in your hands,
A row in spreadsheets, a line that stands,
Performance rankings, a yearly score,
A metric to measure, and nothing more?

Am I the curve on your survey chart,
A data point carved to fit your art,
A psychometric box, a scale-defined,
Reducing my soul to algorithms blind?

You call it "Human" in your name,
Yet where's the person amidst this game?
Where's the story, the dreams, the strife,
The beating heart, the pulse of life?

Do you see the hours I give my best,
The sleepless nights, the unspoken rest?
Do you hear the whispers of fears I hide,

Or the courage it takes to stay and abide?

If all I am is a score to meet,
A trend to track, a form complete,
Then tell me, where is the space for me—
The human you promised in the "HR" to be?

Look beyond the graphs and scales,
Past ratings, reports, and system trails,
See the heart that beats, the hands that toil,
The mind that dreams, the spirit loyal.

For I am more than a number you chart,
I am human, with soul and heart.
So ask yourself—where do we stand,
If humanity slips through HR's hand?

6. The Illusion of Balance

They speak of balance, a measured scale,
Where work and life must not derail.
Yet, when you give your heart and soul,
The weight is theirs to take control.

They say, "Be present," but demand,
Your hours stretch at their command.
A child's soft cry, a fevered night,
Yet duty calls—you mustn't fight.

Sick days linger as silent dreams,
Parental love—dismissed extremes.
A leader's mark, they claim to see,
Yet judge through hours, not dignity.

Balance is always whispered, never freed,
A shadow cast by those in need.
Not measured fair, nor justly spun,
But held by those who've always won.

And so we bend, but must not break,
For balance is the stand we take.
Not given free, nor lightly earned,
But seized, defended, and affirmed.

7. Oh Woman, you cannot succeed!

You have too many obstacles,
Too many chains.
Not questions of competence, not of skill—
But of power, and the weight it remains.
They will resist you,
They will undermine you,
Your strength dismissed as misplaced force.
They will dress their doubts as feedback,
And call their bias - fair discuss!
They who have taken orders from men their whole
careers,
They from you will feel strange.
They will hesitate, they will challenge,
They will question what they could never rearrange.
A man decides—he's confident, bold.
A woman leads—she's too harsh and cold.
A man commands—it's natural, right.
A woman insists—she's picking a fight.
They will ask you to soften,

They will ask to make it easy, to make it light.
They will ask to fit in spaces never built for you,
To dim your fire, mute your fight.
Oh woman, you cannot succeed—
Not because you lack the skill to rise,
But because too many still believe
That power comes only in a male disguise.

And yet — if you do,
If you break through, despite it all,
Then my respect is yours,
Even if no one else's is at all...

8. Work from Home! The New Normal, Now Abnormal

What once was refuge, safe and sound,
A whispered wish, so rarely found.
Work from home, a fleeting grace,
Now a tether we can't erase.

The walls that framed our days with care,
Now mark the lines drawn everywhere.
Is it trust, or what we achieve,
That makes this choice so hard to leave?

The office calls, its hum remains,
The echo of old, familiar chains.
But freedom tasted won't subside,
A quiet strength we hold inside.

Is it presence or the task complete?
Is loyalty judged by the seat or feat?

Or does the mind, unfettered, free,
Find its best where it longs to be?

16

To those who stay, to those who go,
To those who waver, torn below—
May purpose guide, may choice be kind,
May peace reside within your mind.

Let trust be built, not forced, not bound,
Let worth be more than where you're found....
Whatever prevails—structure or flow—
May your best thrive, may not your spirit be low...

9. Promotions - The Chase and the Climb

The chase begins, the fire burns,
A restless heart, the passion churns.
Late nights spent, the dreams take flight,
A title calls—will it be mine?

The whispers grow, the rumors fly,
Hope takes wing, but so does doubt's sigh.
The waiting game, the ticking clock,
Will I stand, or will I walk?

Then it comes—a golden prize,
The rush, the thrill, the lifted highs.
A moment bright, a name now known,
Yet why does it still feel alone?

The cheers will fade, the dust will fall,
The climb will resume, the voices again call.
Another year, another test,
Another chase, really no true rest.

But pause a while—look deep inside,
The real reward is in the ride.
Not in ranks or various names assigned,
But in the strength you've created behind.

Your time will come, none can deny,
When fate aligns, you'll touch the sky.
But till that day, let your courage shine,
For the truest title is always deep inside.

10. Organization Culture, Do you walk the the talk ?

Do you walk the talk, or just let it be,
A promise on paper, but lost in the sea?
Can you do what you say, not just in decree,
But in spirit, in kindness, in true empathy?

Are you the human in HR's embrace,
A voice full of warmth, not a cold interface?
When rules fall short and life gets rough,
Do you bend a little, do you care enough?

Are you a leader who sees past the charts,
Who knows that a team is built from its hearts?
When health must come first, when minds are worn thin,
Do you push them harder, or do you step in?

Are you macro or micro in finance's game?
Do you chase only profit or think past the frame?
Can you weigh a loss, not just for today,
But see how the long road might lead to the way?

Do you reward the fighter who rose from the pain,
Or count just their lapses, dismissing the strain?
Do you judge by the numbers, the tasks left undone,
Or honor resilience—the battle well-won?

Can you be the soft word, the grace,
When policy falters, yet kindness can find space?
Can you see the person, not just the rule,
The weight of their world, the storm they push through?

Can you walk the talk, or is it just a game?
Can you hold to your values when faced with the flame?
For a corporate's culture is important, and not just words
set in stone,
It's the way that you lead where no one feels always
alone.

11. Can You Learn?

Can you learn from the best and the worst alike,
From the guiding stars and the corporate spikes?
From the boss who uplifted, also the one who tore you
down,
From the voice that inspired, the glare, the frown?

Can you see in the chaos a lesson that could unfold,
That leadership isn't just power, but being bold?
Not loud commands, not a fear in disguise,
But knowing when to push, when to rise.

Can you shape your style, distinct yet wise,
Not a borrowed mask, but with truth in your eyes?
Can you sharpen with their feedback, yet hold your own,
Trust your instincts when the seeds are sown?

Can you endure the fire, the weight, the test,
Yet know when to pause, when to rest?
For it's not just a sprint, but a marathon long,
And the strongest don't just run—they grow strong.

Can you stand when the winds turn cold,
Yet bend when the storm takes hold?
Can you lead not just with might,
But with grace, with care, with sight?

For in this world of corporate climb,
The best evolve, but on their time.
So take the lessons, shape your way,
And make yours better than yesterday.

12. The Corner Office Beckons...

The corner office calls your name,
A throne of power, a gilded frame.
Prestige, authority, a seat so high,
Yet beneath it all—you pause, you sigh.

The price is steep, the hours long,
Your time no longer feels your own.
A calendar filled, a mind on fire,
A race of egos, a tightrope wire.

Every choice weighed, each word dissected,
Every move watched, each flaw detected.
The scrutiny sharp, the critics near,
Is the title worth the fear?

You weigh the cost—of nights once free,
Of hobbies lost to strategy.
Of Sundays blurred with Monday's call,
Of boundaries stretched, if there at all.

Yet deep within, a voice rings true,
If this is the love, you always knew.
If you rise and still believe in the flow
That its not for power's fleeting glow.
But for the fire that still remains,
That makes the struggle worth the strain.

And when you stand and take your place,
Not borrowed, nor by hurried chase—
But earned with grit, with love, with might,
You'll know it's yours. And it will feel its *right*.

13. The Gender Pay Gap ?

They say it's a myth, a tale gone stale,
Yet the numbers whisper a different tale.
You see the strides, the ease, the claim,
And wonder—why does mine feel tame?

You work as hard, you think as deep,
Yet watch as others rise and leap.
Is it a lack? A flaw unseen?
Or just a game not built for queens?

The whispers come, soft but sharp—
"You don't need more, you play no part."
"You have a partner, you'll be fine."
"Your work is good, but not like mine."

But know this truth and hold it tight,
Pay Parity isn't a gift—it's a right.
Not a favor, not a plea,
But the mark of true equity.

Your work is precious, your craft is rare,
Even if shaped with a different air.
Not less, not light, not second best,
But worthy—equal, nothing less.

For culture thrives when all can stand,
Not weighed by bias, nor by hand.
So claim your worth, take your space,
For change is slow, but not too late.

14. The Weight of a Reward

Is there reward without a name,
Or fame without a prize to claim?
A silent nod, a whispered cheer,
Or a moment loud for all to hear?

Should it be money, a foreign flight,
A trophy gleaming in the light?
A bunch of flowers, a stage-lit grace,
Or just a seat in the winner's place?

What's the mix that makes it right,
A battle fought in endless night?
For what is fair, what is due,
Is not the same for me and you.

The reward will fade, the moment pass,
Like footprints lost in fleeting grass.
But memory lingers, soft yet strong,
A quiet note, a lasting song.

So, let it not cloud your way,
For triumph lives but for a day.
Rest a while upon your throne,
But never call the road your own.

For ahead there waits another fight,
Another test, another night.
So bear the load, take your stand,
And walk the road with more than a steady hand.

15. The Tightrope for Women..

Do you smile more, speak less,
So they don't call you harsh, or call you a mess?
Do you soften the edges, or dim your light,
So they feel at ease, then you feel right?

Do you downplay the work, make it seem small,
Lest they resent you for having it all?
Do you shrink to fit, nod along,
Hold your fire, though you know they're wrong?

If you were a man, would they still say,
"Too assertive," "too bold," "too much your way"?
Would they ask you to bend, to make it light,
To lead with warmth, not just with might?

But hear me now—don't make yourself small,
You were not built ever to fade at all.
Neither for comfort, nor for ease,
Or to walk on hands or knees for lease.

Be strong, be loud, take your space,
It is yours—you don't need the grace.
Let them wrestle with their view,
You don't owe them a softer *you*.

It will be hard, but stand up tall,
Only then will you break the wall.
For far is not for those who bend,
But for those who dare to *not pretend.*

16. The Monday Question

Does it spark or does it sink,
Does it push you to the brink?
Does a Sunday night bring restless fire,
Or just the weight of lost desire?

Do you lace up, ready to chase,
Or drag your feet to keep the pace?
Does your mind race with plans untold,
Or does it fight, feel tired, feel cold?

Is it always, or just some days,
A fleeting fog, a passing haze?
Or is it deep, a silent call,
A sign that speaks, that says it all?

For if you love it, you will know,
A step that lifts, a heart aglow.
And Mondays won't feel like a fight,
But just the start of something bright.

So listen close, the answer's there,
In how you breathe, in how you care.
For it is work that fuels, that makes you run,
And that turns Mondays into rising suns..

17. The Little Things

A kind word in the hallway's hush,
A smile that sparks a morning rush.
A "Good morning" on a weary day,
A light that pushes the clouds away.

A gentle nod, a thoughtful cheer,
A "Well done" whispered, loud and clear.
A check-in call, a moment spared,
A way to show that someone cared.

The extra step to make it bright,
A meeting planned with warmth and light.
A touch of thought in every space,
The unseen magic, the quiet grace.

An invite sent with heart, not form,
An award speech that can feel *warm.*
The little notes, the extra mile,
The power wrapped inside a smile.

Master this, and you will see,
The corporate world, yet again full of glee.
For work is more than tasks and lore,
It's built on hearts—and on memories *galore.*

18. The Interview

When the moment comes and the stakes are high,
Can you stand tall, can you meet their eye?
Can you quiet the fear, let value shine,
Speak with purpose, make it align?

Can you *hear*, not just *listen*, to what they seek,
Or *listen*, not *hear*, and miss what's unique?
Can you show more than a practiced face,
A glimpse of fire, of depth, of grace?

Are you prepared, or have you left it to fate?
Do you worry, or disengage?
Can you take each question, make it your own,
Adapt, refine, and let your wisdom be shown?

Is your answer rote, just words well-spun,
Or truth that lingers when all is done?
For what they ask is more than skill,
It's who you are, your force, your will.

The result will speak, but know this best—
Do your part, leave to God the rest.
If it's for you, it'll find its way,
Or something greater will come some day.

Trust the universe, trust its space,
For what is yours will know your place.

19. The Salary

It's your bread, your butter, your daily grain,
The fruit of effort, the weight of strain.
But when the day is said and done,
Can you say you *truly* won?

Do you stand before the mirror's gaze,
And claim you've earned your rightful wage?
That time was spent, not lost in vain,
That work was more than just a name?

Did you give as much as you were due,
And take more than what was truly you?
Was each hour fair, was each task met,
With honest toil, and without regret?

For if the scales begin to lean,
Where less is done, but more is seen—
Then know the end is close at hand,
If not today, then soon it will stand.

So work with pride, let worth be shown,
Let effort match the seeds you've sown.
For pay is more than what is wired—
It's proof you gave, you built, you *fired.*

20. Do You See Them?

Do you see the one who holds the door,
Who stands all day, yet is ignored?
The hands that brew your morning cup,
The quiet ones that lift you up?

Do you notice the guard at dawn's first light,
Keeping watch through the silent night?
The receptionist with a ready smile,
Who greets by name, who stays a while?

The ones who clean, who set the space,
Who add the warmth, the unseen grace?
The silent gears that make it run,
Whose work is done but never sung?

In this world of ladders high,
Where names are known, yet some pass by,
May you pause, may you see,
For kindness shapes what you be.

For power fades, but hearts remain,
And what you give is what you gain.
So let no title make you blind,
May you be a human first—warm and kind.

21. Rest in Peace, oh Bell Curve

May the bell curve rest in peace,
Its time is done, let it release.
A tool once hailed, now worn and weak,
A model flawed, unfair, oblique.

Did it see the work we gave?
The countless hours, the risks we braved?
Or did it box, did it confine,
Dimming stars that dared to shine?

Not all can fit its rigid line,
Not all should peak, then just decline.
For growth is more than ranked success,
And talent thrives beyond *percentiles' guess.*

So let new models take the stage,
With fairness set on every page.
Where effort counts, where people grow,
Not crushed beneath a curve we know.

May the bell curve rest in peace,
Its time is done—let it release.
For work deserves a better way,
Where every voice has room to stay.

22. The Corporate Dichotomy

Be passionate, yet stay detached,
Hold the fire, but surely don't get scratched.
Care too much, and you may burn,
Care too little, and none will turn.

Be fierce in your fight, yet calm in your stance,
Know when to lead, when to enhance.
Too hot-headed, and you can fall,
Too cold-blooded, you'll lose it all.

Speak with force, yet weigh each word,
Be sharp, yet soft—let both be heard.
Push ahead, but know restraint,
Too much zeal can leave a taint.

Win the war, but not the cost,
For battles blind, can leave you lost.
The trick is knowing when to stay,
And when to walk the other way.

So hold the heat, yet breathe it cool,
Know the game, but not as a fool.
For it is balance that shapes the ones who thrive,
And keeps the heart of our work alive.

23. Mind the Mind

Respect the weight the mind must bear,
The silent struggles, the hidden wear.
Not all wounds are seen, not all cries are loud,
Some battles rage beneath the crowd.

See the signs—the weary glance,
The lost-in-thought, the hollow stance.
The fire dimmed, the laughter strained,
The burden carried, often not deigned.

Help your team to walk it through,
A kind word can change the view.
A pause, a space, a moment's grace,
Can bring back light to a shadowed face.

Help your boss, they bear it too,
Pressure mounts at every view.
Leaders can stumble, leaders can break,
They, too, need hands that lift, not take.

For we are only as strong as our health,
Not just our targets, not just our wealth.
So mind the mind, and let care begin,
For a workplace thrives when hearts can win.

24. The Power of No

True power isn't in chasing long,
Nor holding tight to where you *belong*.
It isn't in titles, in perks well-earned,
But knowing when the tide has turned.

To say *no* to the role once sought,
The dream that once defined your thought.
The offer grand, the corner seat,
Yet knowing now—it's not your feat.

For you have built, you have grown,
Your skills, your choices, now your own.
No longer bound by past pursuit,
You choose not the fear, but the deeper truth.

For *yes* is easy, but *no* is might,
It confirms that you've scaled a different height.
And when you turn, and let it go,
That's when you own the *power of no*.

25. The Pain and the Path

Does it pain to leave the home behind,
To trade the warm hugs for the daily grind?
Does the long road wear you thin,
As the city swallows, the race begins?

Does it pinch—the need to earn,
The weight of duty, the endless churn?
Does the ache of hours gone,
Make you wonder where you belong?

But know this—you *must* go through,
For life gives burdens to *all*, not few.
Each bears a cross, unseen, unknown,
Yet step by step, the path is shown.

There may be no balance, no perfect way,
Yet take it one breath, one task, one day.
For even in struggle, in toil, in strife,
You carve your name into the heights of life.

And one day soon, when you look behind,
You'll see the climb was worth the grind.
The minutes spent, the hours you gave,
Have built the heights none else could pave.

26. Know This to Be True

After you leave, after you're gone,
The emails will fade, the calls move on.
Your name may linger in halls for a while,
A whisper, a mention, a fleeting smile.

On your 80th, who will recall
The meetings you led, the decks, the sprawl?
The titles, the targets, the deadlines tight,
The late-night battles, the corporate fight?

The future will come, fresh and free,
With no space for the past that once was *thee.*
And if it was only for butter alone,
Will you look back and still feel at home?

For time will fade, as time must do,
And what will only matter is *you* to *you.*
So make it a life, not just a race,
A story of joy, of heart, of grace.

27. Women Who Rise

A rarity now, but one day bright,
May they lead with equal right.
No chains of doubt, no bias deep,
No glass to break, no heights to keep.

May they rise with voices strong,
Their style embraced, where they belong.
Not shaped to fit, not trimmed to please,
But leading brave and bold, with fearless ease.

May pay be fair, not fought in vain,
Not lesser worth, nor lesser gain.
May dues be given, not begrudged,
For talent speaks where none should judge.

May life's transitions find them space,
Not held behind, but met with grace.
With hands that lift at every stage,
Support that grows, not fades with age.

A rarity now, but not for long,
May change be swift, may roots be strong.
For when we stand, and rise as one,
The world will know—yes, her time has come.

28. The Story of a Career

No path of a career is perfect, smooth, or straight,
No climb of it is free of toil or fate.
What seems like gold from far away,
May hide its cracks and make you sway.

Each tale of triumph, bold and bright,
Has its share of a stormy night.
For every peak, there was a valley deep,
For every win, there was a loss to keep.

The sinking lows, the weary stride,
The doubts that creep, the dreams that hide.
Yet through it all, one day the highs will shine,
The moments will be sweet, the victories fine.

So chase not dreams that *seem* just right,
But those that set your soul alight.
Where the mind and spirit, body whole,
Find purpose and passion—*that's* the goal.

Keep preparing to rise and grow,
One day the world will surely know.
A toast, a tale, your journey will be told,
Of a life fulfilled—not just in gold.

29. Lessons from Indra Nooyi

She walked the halls with grace and might,
A vision clear and a guiding light.
From boardroom walls to world of acclaim,
She carved her path, she changed the gender game.

She taught us strength in every stride,
That dreams can grow tall and paired with pride.
To lead with a heart, yet hold your ground,
To lift up the voices all around.

She showed that growth is never fast,
That every step you must hold steadfast.
That learning never finds an end,
And every fall can help you mend.

She taught that home and work must blend,
Yet if balance bends, it won't transcend.
To honour our roots, yet rise and soar,
To break the mould, and build so much more.

So, walk ahead with courage like her bright,
With wisdom sharp and heart in sight.
For those who lead with truth and grace,
Like her, will leave a lasting trace.

30. Hold On, the Tide Will Turn

When you are weary, lost, and drained,
When all you've given feels in vain.
When the weight you bear is hard to hold,
And dreams once bright now seem too old.

When toil and struggle make you swear,
When ego bruises and none seems fair.
When tides rise high, against your will,
And standing firm takes all your skill.

When quitting feels the only way,
When doubts cloud every step of the day.
When whispers turn to storms so loud,
And shadows chase you to make you bowed.

When politics entangle tight,
And nothing seems to turn out right.
When doors won't open, paths won't show,
And hope is distant, dim, with many a foe.

Hold on, my friend, don't let it slide,
The darkest hour always births the tide.
For if you've walked with your truth in hand,
The waves *will* shift, and you *will* withstand.

31. The Cost of Professional Dishonesty

It starts as whispers, slight and small,
A hidden lie, Being quiet on a call.
A number tweaked, a truth withheld,
A promise made, but never held.

It spreads like cracks within the walls,
Ignored too long, the structure falls.
What seemed so harmless, just a bend,
Becomes the norm, a means, an end.

A culture built on half-truth's game,
Will one day bear the weight of shame.
For trust once lost is hard to gain,
And all that's built will fall in vain.

The leaders turn, pretend, delay,
But cracks don't heal, they can't find their way.
And when the dust begins to clear,
The cost is more than it appears.

So mind the truth, and, uphold what's right,
For strength is built in the open light.
An honest path may rise up slow,
But it's the only one where success will grow.

32. The Need of Learning

What you knew, once sharp and bright,
May fade away, lose its light.
The world moves fast, the tides will change,
What once was certain feels so strange.

The skills you held, the truths you swore,
May not hold weight like once before.
Yet learning never goes in vain,
Each lesson shapes what you retain.

Adapt, evolve, invest in *you*,
For growth is found in all you do.
Not all you learn is meant to stay,
But wisdom knows what to relay.

The agile mind, the willing hand,
Will always find new ground to stand.
For never was a lesson lost,
If it was learned—no matter the cost.

33. Rhymes of Corporate Crimes, Verses from the Corner Office

The corner office, high and grand,
A throne of power, built on sand.
Yet whispers echo through the walls,
Of silent deals and quiet falls.

The numbers shine, the charts ascend,
Yet truth may bend, a means to end.
A bonus sways, a line is blurred,
A choice is made—no questions stirred.

The brightest minds, the sharpest suits,
Yet greed can rot the strongest roots.
The race for more, the silent war,
Where values slip behind locked doors.

Yet not all corners cast a shade,
Some stand tall, unbent, unfrayed.
For power's weight is not the crime,
It's how it's used, *or left behind.*

So lead with truth, let honor stay,
Let no dark rhymes mark your way.
For in the end, when stories close,
It's *how* you led that truly shows.

34. Meetings and Calendars

A calendar full, from dawn to night,
Does it mean you've reached the height?
A seat in rooms, a voice so loud,
Yet are you lost within the crowd?

The meetings stack, the time slips by,
A rush, a race, no space to try.
Decisions made in fleeting thought,
But was the depth, the meaning sought?

Does solving more bring true delight,
Or just the blur of fading light?
Is there a pause, a space to dream,
Or just the pull of the next regime?

For wisdom grows in time and space,
Not in the endless meeting chase.
Not in the rush from door to door,
But in the time to think, do much more.

So clear the noise, make room to *be*,
For thought, for depth, for clarity.
A mindless dash will wear you thin,
But space to *think and do*—that's where you win.

35. Is It Lonely at the Top?

They said the climb would bring you pride,
A view so grand, the world so wide.
Yet as you stand where few have been,
You pause and ask—where are *my* kin?

The voices fade, the air is thin,
Decisions weigh so deep within.
The laughter once so free and bright,
Now echoes softly in the night.

The burdens grow, the wins feel light,
Applause fades fast, gone out of sight.
For every step, a cost was paid,
In friendships lost, in plans that delayed.

Yet lonely is a path *you* shape,
A fate not set, a choice to make.
For if you lift as you ascend,
You'll find a hand, a voice, a friend.

So lead with heart, let warmth remain,
For power fades, but love sustains.
And when you stand atop that height,
May it be filled with many a delight.

36. The Whispered Game of Gossips

The murmurs rise, the stories spin,
A tale retold, a slanted grin.
Harmless chatter, so it seems,
A fleeting laugh, a bond redeemed.

But words take flight, they twist, they turn,
What once was small begins to burn.
A fact misplaced, a name entwined,
A careless jest, a mark unkind.

Is it insight, is it noise?
A way to stay, to have a voice?
Yet balance *must* be held with care,
For whispers leave a lasting air.

No crafted post, no work so grand,
Can mend the stain of a loose hand.
For in these halls, what stays, what flies,
Is not just truth—but how it's tied.

So mind the words, the tales you weave,
For what you spread, you shall receive.
And long beyond your finest hour,
Your name will hold that whispered power.

37. The Edge of Growth

You toil through nights, you race through days,
Lost in meetings, caught in maze.
The emails flood, the calls don't end,
The ladder climbs, rewards ascend.

The lure is strong—the title, the pay,
The rise feels grand, at least today.
But pause and ask—what stays, what goes?
What truly lasts, what truly grows?

For those who win beyond the now,
Are those who learn, who ask the *how?*
A course, a book, a skill refined,
A sharper edge, a brighter mind.

The world will shift, the trends will change,
What's known today may soon seem strange.
Yet those who grow, who choose to learn,
Will find their place at every turn.

So take the time, invest in *you*,
For knowledge builds what titles *can't* do.
Upskill, evolve, stay sharp, stay wise,
For only then will you truly rise.

38. The Perfect Exit

A handshake firm, a speech so bright,
A room that glows in the farewell light.
Fond memories wrapped in a warm embrace,
A chapter closed with love and grace.

Or silent steps, no words, no cheer,
A name erased, once held so dear.
A quiet nod, a heavy sigh,
No looking back, just passing by.

Or a golden deal, a future free,
The purse is full, but what will be?
No desk, no mails, no daily call,
And does the heart still crave it all?

Some leave in joy, some leave in pain,
Some walk away, some still remain.
Yet every step, so right or wrong,
Becomes a verse in your own song.

So as you go, just hold this true—
The path ahead *belongs to you.*
And whether bright or bittersweet now,
The best awaits if that's what you sow.

39. The Office Family

We start as strangers, side by side,
Through deadlines met and tasks we need to abide.
A bond is built, a laugh is shared,
A silent vow— our hearts are bared.

The coffee chats, the midnight calls,
The lifted hands when someone falls.
Through wins and losses, highs and lows,
A second home, a warmth grows.

But time will shift, and roles will change,
The ties once close may feel estranged.
A friend, now just a name and face,
A colleague now, in time and place.

For friendships here are rare, but bright,
A fleeting star, a guiding light.
Yet kindness lingers, memories stay,
The mark we leave won't fade away.

So build it strong, this space, this crew,
For what we give shapes what we do.
And if we make it good for all,
Then work will not feel like *just* a call.

40. The Many Faces of a Boss

The *Visionary*, eyes set on far,
A guiding light, a rising star.
They push, they dream, they show the way,
Yet leave you room to have your say.

The *Taskmaster*, firm and cold,
Numbers first, results needed bold.
Deadlines sharp, no space to stray,
Yet in their fire, you find your way.

The *Mentor*, wise, with words so kind,
Sees your spark, and shapes your mind.
With patience rare, they lift you high,
A steady hand, a watchful eye.

The *Ghost*, so absent, lost in thought,
Decisions pending, battles you fought.
A name, a title, but not much more,
A leader missing from the floor.

The *Politician*, smooth yet sly,
A charming grin, a practiced eye.
They climb, they scheme, they play the game,
Yet leave you standing without any fame.

The *Tyrant*, so loud, demands control,
Breaks your will, yet fuels your soul.
For in their storm, you learn to stand,
To find your voice, to take command.

And then there's one, so rare, so true,
Who leads with their heart, who walks with you.
Not just a boss, but one who cares,
A name you'll speak in your grateful prayers.

But one day time will turn, the tables will shift,
One day, you'll hold the leadership gift.
So ask yourself—when all is through,
Which one of these will become *you*?

41. The Weight of Bias

She walks in strong, her head held high,
Yet unseen forces whisper *why?*
Too bold, too soft, too much, too less,
A woman's path—always an unfair test.

The Likeability Trap, a quiet snare,
Be warm, be firm—but don't you dare
To be *too* assertive, *too* in control,
For you'll watch respect slip through the hole.

The Motherhood Myth, a tale so old,
Will she return? Can she uphold?
A mind that's sharp, a heart so wide,
Yet judged before she steps inside.

The Pay Gap Chasm, silent deep,
Where numbers lie and secrets keep.
She works, she shines, yet not the same,
A smaller check, always a bigger shame.

The Leadership Lens, so tight, so small,
Men may command, but she must *call*.
Her power viewed with wary eyes,
While others rise, she justifies.

Yet still she must climb, she must claim her space,
She must bend the rules, set the pace.
For though the weight is hard to bear,
She must stand, she must dare .

42. The Corporate Maze: A Team of Many

A team is built of many kinds,
With different hearts and different minds.
In this maze where careers are spun,
Each plays a part, each has work to be done.

The *Go-Getter*, eager and bright,
Takes on tasks with boundless might.
They race ahead, they set the pace,
Yet sometimes forget to leave a trace.

The *Silent Worker*, steady, true,
Not one for noise, yet much they do.
No grand displays, no claims of fame,
But without them, all's not the same.

The *Idea Machine*, a restless soul,
With thoughts so wild, beyond control.
Their visions soar, they spark the flame,
Yet follow-through is not their game.

The *Diplomat*, so smooth, so wise,
Navigates storms with careful ties.
They calm the fire, they bridge the gap,
With words that heal and a gentle tap.

The *Lone Wolf*, a force apart,
Prefers to work with head, not a heart.
Efficient, sharp, they get the things done,
Yet miss the joy of teams as one.

The *Taskmaster*, strict and keen,
Keeps the deadlines crisp and clean.
A checklist rules their every day,
No room for fun, just work and stay.

The *Firefighter*, last-minute knight,
Thrives in chaos, finds the light.
Crisis calls, they jump right in,
But why the fire? Where to begin?

And then there's one, the *Team Guide*,
Who lifts, inspires, walks beside.
They lead, they listen, they help you grow,
A kindred soul in highs and lows.

A team is more than just a name,

More than targets, more than fame.
Find your part, play it true,
For in this maze, *they need you too.*

43. The Performance Appraisal: A Corporate Reckoning

The year has passed, the numbers stand,
A ledger tallied by unseen hands.
The wins, the toil, the silent fights,
Now cast in scores and measured in bytes.

The *self-review*, a hopeful start,
A tale you tell with honest heart.
Yet in the room where verdicts fall,
Do they see your all in all?

The *feedback round*, a mirror bright,
Reflects your strengths, reveals the light.
Yet shadows lurk in words unsaid,
A single flaw—where all eyes will tread.

The *bell curve looms*, its edges tight,
Not all can shine, though all took flight.

Some will rise and claim the prize,
While others will watch with tired eyes.

84

And when it's done, the dust will clear,
Was it fair, or built on fear?
Yet know this truth, beyond the frame—
No rating will *ever* define your name.

So take the praise, take the scars,
Wear them proud, like battle stars.
For growth is more than numbers tallied—
It's in the strength with which you rallied.

44. Excellence & Power: The Corporate Tools

Excellence comes with *Excel's* might,
Rows and columns, crisp and tight.
Numbers dance, formulas flow,
A world of logic built to show.

Power comes from *PowerPoint*, bold and bright,
Slides that tell a story right.
Charts that soar, words that shine,
A vision crafted, sharp and fine.

One builds the case with structured grace,
The other sways with style and pace.
Data and drama, side by side,
The corporate world's eternal guide.

Yet know this truth, beyond the screens,
It's not the tools but the hands unseen.
For skill is more than decks and sheets—
It's the mind that makes them meet and beat

45. The HR Survey: Voices in the Void

An email pings, a link appears,
"Your feedback matters!"—year by year.
A few short clicks, a box to type,
A chance to voice, to hope, to gripe.

"Do you feel valued?" "Do you feel heard?"
Tick the scale, but weigh each word.
For honesty feels like a dangerous game,
When the past has left things much the same.

Anonymous, yet doubts arise,
"Will they know? Will it be wise?"
Speak too much, and risk the glare,
Say too little—does anyone care?

Yet numbers can twist, and words can be spun,
Graphs will glow, but what is done?
Is truth embraced, or wrapped to fit,
A narrative that's cleanly knit?

A tool so sharp, a blade so fine,
To cut through mist, or blur the line.
Use it well, maybe trust will grow,
Misuse it, and all will know.

So ask, but act, and make it right,
Let voices rise beyond the site.
For surveys mean not what we say,
But *what we can change* along the way.

46. Diversity, Inclusion & Equity: More Than Just Words

A seat at the table, yet none at the head,
A voice in the room, yet nothing is said.
The meeting flows, decisions are made,
Did they listen, or was it a charade?

A mother returns, her heart in two,
Balancing work, yet doubted anew.
"Will she cope? Can she stay?"
A silent bias clouds her way.

A name on a résumé, bold and bright,
Yet passes unseen at the hiring site.
"Not a culture fit," the panel sighs,
A hidden wall behind their eyes.

A wheelchair waits at the office door,
Steps that stand like times of yore.

Talent locked in a world unfair,
When access is *not* only a flight of stairs.

Diversity shines when all can thrive,
Inclusion breathes when all feel alive.
Equity means a bridge is laid,
So no one's worth is left to fade.

Not just policies, not just plans,
But choices made with mindful hands.
For change is only real when all can see,
A workplace that was built for *you* and *me to be*

47. The Many Faces at Work

The *Tech Diva*, bold and bright,
Building code deep into the night.
With every bug, they tracks and slay,
To shape the future in brilliant ways.

The *Finance Wizard*, sharp and keen,
Numbers dancing on their screen.
Balancing books, making it right,
Turning chaos into deep insight.

The *HR Buddy*, warm and wise,
A guiding hand, a listening eye to size .
With every hire, every care,
They build a culture, fair and rare.

The *Admin Caretaker*, steady, true,
Keeping the wheels from turning blue.
From desks to doors, from lights to air,
A silent force, for you always there.

The *IT Geek*, in shadows deep,
Guarding data while others sleep.
Cables, networks, servers hum,
A fortress strong—no threats to come.

The *Treasury Caretaker*, wise and bold,
Counting coins and watching gold.
Investing, saving, watching flows,
Ensuring that the money grows.

The *Product Creator*, dreamer's mind,
New ideas, the rarest kind.
Designing things that change the game,
Turning visions ever into fame.

The *Marketing Buzz Maker*, loud and proud,
Making noise for every crowd.
Telling stories, selling dreams,
Giving brands their brightest gleam.

The *Service Champ*, hearts so wide,
Solving problems, side by side.
With every call, with every care,
They show the world that *we can bear.*

Yet, at the heart of all we do,
One story rings, one voice shines through.

The *Customer*—the start, the end,
The one we must serve, and should be our truest friend.

92

48. Careerathon: The Marathon of Work

The gun goes off, the race is set,
A fresh new start with no regret.
Eyes are bright, the road is wide,
Dreams and goals run side by side.

The *early miles* are light and free,
Learning, growing, eager to be.
Each step builds, each lesson stays,
Fueling fire for the future days.

Then *midway comes*, the hill is steep,
Pressure mounts, the climb is deep.
Deadlines chase, the weight is real,
You still push ahead for that steal.

The *wall* appears at mile fifteen,
Doubt and burnout in between.
"Can I go on? Should I slow?"
A moment to pause, but not to let go.

With the second wind, a newfound pace,
Wisdom shines upon your face.
Skills are honed, instincts are true,
The road ahead is clearer too.

The *final stretch*, the homeward run,
A legacy built, a race well done.
Looking back, through the highs and lows,
The finish line is where *you* drove.

A career's not a sprint, but long and wide,
Paced with grit and growing stride.
So run it well, with all heart and cheer,
For every step makes the journey dear.

49. The Endless Meeting

The clock strikes nine, the room fills in,
Fresh with hope, where do we begin?
A slide appears, a voice takes flight,
Another meeting— ohh buckle tight.

Cups of coffee, growing cold,
A story stale, again retold.
Twiddling thumbs, a restless sigh,
Staring blankly, wondering why.

The biscuits come, a fleeting cheer,
No stretch, no break, still stuck in here.
The words go round in practiced spin,
Rhetoric thick, yet nothing sinks in.

A motion picture, we play no part,
A silent spectator, numb at the heart.
The time ticks , the walls don't bend,
Will this ever, ever end?

A thought escapes—so sharp, so free, so beat
"Life could be great, but not in this seat."
Yet we nod, and yet we stay,
Lost in more meetings, day by day.

50. Resilience in Corporate Life

The tides will rise, the winds will shake,
The road will bend, the bridges break.
The weight of deadlines, the silent strife,
This is the rhythm of a corporate life.

The deals may fail, the plans may go wrong,
The meetings drag, the days will feel long.
Yet through it all, you stand up tall,
For every stumble, you still walk, it's your call.

The words may sting, the doubts may creep,
The nights be restless, the falls be deep.
But steel is forged in a fire's embrace,
And strength is born through trials faced.

So rise again, reset your pace,
No storm can dim your inner grace.
For those who stand through thick and thin,
Are those who fight—and *always win*

www.ingramcontent.com/pod-product-compliance
Lightning Source LLC
La Vergne TN
LVHW011033200726
843509LV00011B/1268